# Rembrandt

# *Rembrandt*

an exhibition sponsored by the
American Express Foundation.

Gemäldegalerie, Staatliche Museen,
at the Altes Museum, Berlin
    Paintings: 12 September—10 November 1991
    Etchings:　12 September—10 November 1991
    Drawings: 12 September—27 October 1991

Rijksmuseum, Amsterdam
    Paintings: 4 December 1991—1 March 1992
    Etchings:　4 December 1991—1 March 1992
    Drawings: 4 December 1991—19 January 1992

The National Gallery, London
    Paintings: 26 March—24 May 1992
    Etchings:　26 March—24 May 1992

British Museum, London
    Drawings: 26 March—4 August 1992

een tentoonstelling onderstaund door de
American Express Foundation.

Gemäldegalerie, Staatliche Museen,
in het Altes Museen, Berlijn
    Schilderijen: 12 september—10 november 1991
    Ets:　　　　　12 september—10 november 1991
    Tekeningen: 12 september—27 oktober 1991

Rijksmuseum, Amsterdam
    Schilderijen: 4 december 1991—1 maart 1992
    Ets:　　　　　4 december 1991—1 maart 1992
    Tekeningen: 4 december 1991—19 januari 1992

The National Gallery, Londen
    Schilderijen: 26 maart—24 mei 1992
    Ets:　　　　　26 maart—24 mei 1992

British Museum, Londen
    Tekeningen: 26 maart—4 augustus 1992

eine Ausstellung gefördert von der
American Express Foundation.

Gemäldegalerie, Staatliche Museen,
im Alten Museen, Berlin
    Gemälde:　　　12 September—10 November 1991
    Radierung:　　12 September—10 November 1991
    Zeichnungen: 12 September—27 Oktober 1991

Rijksmuseum, Amsterdam
    Gemälde:　　　4 Dezember 1991—1 März 1992
    Radierung:　　4 Dezember 1991—1 März 1992
    Zeichnungen: 4 Dezember 1991—19 Januar 1992

The National Gallery, London
    Gemälde:　　　26 März—24 Mai 1992
    Radierung:　　26 März—24 Mai 1992

British Museum, London
    Zeichnungen: 26 März—4 August 1992

exposition organisée avec le concours de
l'American Express Foundation.

Gemäldegalerie, Staatliche Museum,
au Altes Museum, Berlin
    Peintures: 12 septembre—10 novembre 1991
    Eau-forte: 12 septembre—10 novembre 1991
    Dessins:　 12 septembre—27 octobre 1991

Rijksmuseum, Amsterdam
    Peintures: 4 décembre 1991—1 mars 1992
    Eau-forte: 4 décembre 1991—1 mars 1992
    Dessins:　 4 décembre 1991—19 janvier 1992

The National Gallery, Londres
    Peintures: 26 mars—24 mai 1992
    Eau-forte: 26 mars—24 mai 1992

British Museum, Londres
    Dessins:　 26 mars—4 août 1992

# Rembrandt

## The Master and his Workshop
## Der Meister und seine Werkstatt
## de meester en zijn werkplaats
## Le Maître et son Atelier

ADDRESSES
ADRESSEN
ADRESSES

National Gallery Publications, London

Universe

*The Shell,* 1650, Etching, 9.7 x 13.2 cm. London, British Museum.

*Die Muschel,* 1650, Radierung, 9,7 x 13,2cm. London, British Museum.

*De schelp,* 1650, Ets, 9,7 x 13,2 cm. Londen, British Museum.

*La Coquille,* 1650, Eau-forte, 9,7 x 13,2 cm. Londres, British Museum.

Published by
UNIVERSE
300 Park Avenue South
New York, NY 10010

Printed in Hong Kong

Rembrandt. f.1650.

# Rembrandt

*F*or the first time in history, four major museums in Berlin, Amsterdam and London are hosting a comprehensive exhibition of paintings, drawings and etchings by the Dutch master, Rembrandt. The Gemäldegalerie, Staatliche Museum, Berlin; Rijksmuseum, Amsterdam; The National Gallery, London; and the British Museum, London, have come together to organize this extraordinary exhibition, bringing works from their rich Rembrandt holdings as well as from public and private collections worldwide.

This exhibition is particularly timely in view of the unprecedented work of the Rembrandt Research Project which, for more than twenty years, has been studying important scientific and art historical aspects about Rembrandt and his work. As a result of this inquiry, the exhibition reveals more about the artist than has ever been known before and enables visitors to appreciate more fully the genius of the artist himself.

*Z*um ersten Mal in der Geschichte, präsentieren vier Museen größter Bedeutung in Berlin, Amsterdam und London eine umfassende Ausstellung von Gemälden, Zeichnungen und Radierungen des holländischen Meisters Rembrandt. Die Gemäldegalerie, Staatliche Museen, Berlin; Rijksmuseum, Amsterdam; The National Gallery, London; und das British Museum, London, haben sich zusammengeschlossen, um diese außergewöhnliche Ausstellung, mit Werken aus ihren eigenen reichhaltigen Rembrandt Sammlungen und aus öffentlichen und privaten Kollektionen weltweit, zu veranstalten.

Diese Ausstellung findet genau zum rechten Zeitpunkt statt, im Hinblick auf die einmalige Arbeit des Rembrandt Research Project, welches seit mehr als zwanzig Jahren die wichtigsten wissenschaftlichen und kunsthistorischen Aspekte über Rembrandt und seine Arbeiten erforscht. Aus dieser studie resultierend, enthüllt die Ausstellung mehr als jemals zuvor über den Künstler und ermöglicht es den Besuchern um so mehr, den Genius des Meisters zu schätzen.

# Rembrandt

*H*et is voor het eerst dat vier van de belangrijkste musea in Berlijn, Amsterdam en Londen samen een veelomvattende tentoonstelling presenteren van schilderijen, tekeningen en etsen van Rembrandt. De Gemäldegalerie, Staatliche Museen, Berlijn; het Rijksmuseum, Amsterdam; The National Gallery, Londen; en het British Museum, Londen, hebben hun krachten gebundeld om deze buitengewone tentoonstelling te organiseren, met werken uit hun indrukwekkende Rembrandt collecties en uit openbare en particuliere verzamelingen van over de hele wereld.

Deze tentoonstelling is bijzonder actueel gezien het belangwekkende werk van het Rembrandt Research Project, dat al meer dan twintig jaar een studie maakt van de technische en kunsthistorische aspecten van Rembrandt's werk. Dankzij dit onderzoek kan de tentoonstelling meer over Rembrandt onthullen dan ooit tevoren en kunnen bezoekers zijn kunstenaarschap ten volle leren kennen.

*P*our la première fois, quatre grands musées—à Berlin, à Amsterdam et à Londres—organisent une exposition sur l'ensemble des peintures, des dessins et des eaux-fortes du maître hollandais, Rembrandt. La Gemäldegalerie, Staatliche Museum, Berlin; Rijksmuseum, Amsterdam; The National Gallery, Londres; et le British Museum, Londres, se sont réunis pour présenter cette exposition importante, y apportant des oeuvres de leurs riches collections comme de celles, publiques et privés, de par le monde.

Cette exposition est particulièrement opportune à la lumière du travail sans précédent du projet de recherche sur Rembrandt ("Rembrandt Research Project") qui, depuis plus de vingt ans, étudie l'homme et l'oeuvre à l'aide de la technique moderne et des outils de l'histoire de l'art. Par suite de ces recherches cette exposition met à jour pour l'appréciation du visiteur des aspects jusqu'ici inconnus du génie de cet artiste.

# A

# A

*The Standard-Bearer,* 1636, Canvas, 118.8 x 96.8 cm. Paris, private collection.

*Der Fahnenträger,* 1636, Leinwand, 118,8 x 96,8 cm. Paris, Privatsammlung.

*De vaandeldrager,* 1636, Doek, 118,8 x 96,8 cm. Parijs, particuliere verzameling.

*Le Porte-drapeau,* 1636, Toile, 118,8 x 96,8 cm. Paris, collection privée.

B

*A Woman standing with a Candle,* c.1631, Pen and brown ink with brown and grey wash, heightened with white, 18.1 x 13.2 cm. London, British Museum. Purchased with the Malcolm Collection, 1895-9-15-1268

*Stehende Frau mit Kerze,* um 1631, Feder mit brauner Tinte, braun und grau laviert, weiss gehöht, 18,1 x 13,2 cm. London, British Museum. Erworben mit der Malcolm Sammlung, 1895-9-15-1268

*Staande vrouw met een kaars,* ca.1631, Pen in bruin, bruin en grijs gewassen, met wit gehoogd, 18,1 x 13,2 cm. Londen, British Museum. Verworven met de Malcolm verzameling, 1895-9-15-1268

*Femme debout avec bougie,* vers 1631, Plume et encre brune, rehaussé de blanc, 18,1 x 13,2 cm. Londres, British Museum. Achat faisant parti de la collection Malcolm, 1895-9-15-1268

# B

---

*The Sampling Officials of the Amsterdam Drapers' Guild (The 'Staalmeesters'),* 1662, Canvas, 191.5 x 279 cm. Amsterdam, Rijksmuseum (On loan from the City of Amsterdam). Inv. No. C6

*Die Staalmeesters,* 1662, Leinwand, 191,5 x 279 cm. Amsterdam, Rijksmuseum (Leihgabe der Stadt Amsterdam). Inv. Nr. C6

*De staalmeesters,* 1662, Doek, 191,5 x 279 cm. Amsterdam, Rijksmuseum (bruikleen van de stad Amsterdam). Inv. Nr. C6

*Les Syndics de la guilde des drapiers d'Amsterdam (Les Staalmeesters),* 1662, Toile, 191,5 x 279 cm. Amsterdam, Rijksmuseum, prêt de la Ville d'Amsterdam). inv. n°. C6

**B**

Two Women teaching a Child
to Walk, c.1635-37, Red chalk
on rough grey paper, 10.3 x
12.8 cm. London, British
Museum, Bequeathed by
George Salting, 1910-2-12-187

*Zwei Frauen die einem Kind
das Gehen lehren,* um 1635-
37, Rote Kreide auf grauem
Papier, 10,3 x 12,8 cm. London, British Museum,
Vermächtnis George Salting,
1910-2-12-187

*Twee vrouwen die een kind
leren lopen,* ca.1635-37, Rood
krijt op ruw grijs papier, 10,3
x 12,8 cm. Londen, Brit-
ish Museum, Legaat George
Salting, 1910-2-12-187

*Deux Femmes apprenant à
marcher à un enfant,* vers
1635-37, Craie rouge sur
papier gris, 10,3 x 12,8 cm.
Londres, British Museum,
Legs de George Salting, 1910-
2-12-187

# C

**The rich Man from the Parable,** 1627, Panel, 32 x 42.5 cm. Berlin, Staatliche Museen Preussischer Kulturbesitz, Gemäldegalerie. No. 828 D

*Der Reiche aus dem Gleichnis vom reichen Toren,* 1627, Holz, 32 x 42,5 cm. Berlin, Staatliche Museen Preußischer Kulturbesitz, Gemäldegalerie. Nr. 828 D

*De rijkaard uit de "Gelijkenis van de rijke dwaas",* 1627, Paneel, 32 x 42,5 cm. Berlijn, Staatliche Museen Preussischer Kulturbesitz, Gemäldegalerie. nr. 828 D

*Le Changeur,* 1627, Bois, 32 x 42,5 cm. Berlin, Staatliche Museen Preussischer Kulturbesitz, Gemäldegalerie. 828 D

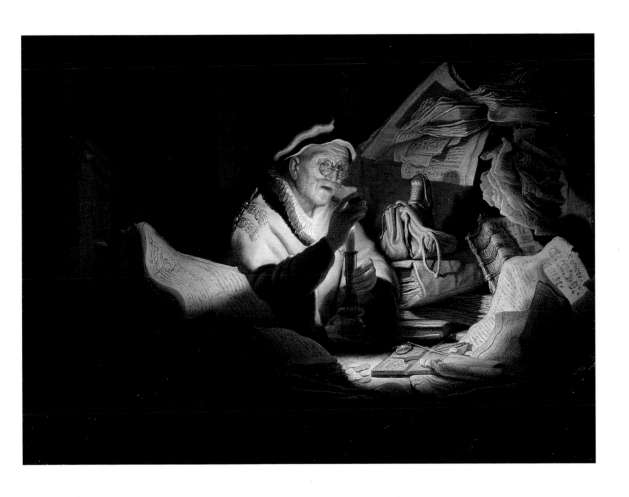

*The Art Dealer, Clement de Jonghe,* 1651, Etching, 20.6 x 16.1 cm. London, British Museum.

*Clement de Jonghe, Kupfer-stichverleger,* 1651, Radie-rung, 20,6 x 16,1 cm. London, British Museum.

*De kunsthandelaar Clement de Jonghe,* 1651, Ets, 20,6 x 16,1 cm. Londen, British Museum.

*Le Marchand d'art Clément de Jonghe,* 1651, Eau-forte, 20,6 x 16,1 cm. Londres, British Museum.

# C

*Three Studies of a Bearded Man on Crutches and a Woman,* c.1632-34, Pen and brown ink, 15.2 x 18.5 cm. London, British Museum. Bequeathed by C.M. Cracherode, 1799

*Drei Studien von einem Mann mit Bart auf Krücken und einer Frau,* um 1632-34, Feder mit brauner Tinte, 15,2 x 18,5 cm. London, British Museum. Vermächtnis C.M. Cracherode, 1799

*Drie studies van een man op krukken, en een studie van een vrouw,* ca.1632-34, Pen in bruin, 15,2 x 18,5 cm. Londen, British Museum. Legaat C.M. Cracherode, 1799

*Trois études d'un homme barbu avec béquilles et d'une femme,* vers 1632-34, Plume et encre brune, 15,2 x 18,5 cm. Londres, British Museum. Legs de C.M. Cracherode, 1799

# D

*Ecce Homo,* 1634, Paper on canvas, 54.5 x 44.5 cm. London, The National Gallery. Inv. No. 1400

*Ecce homo,* 1634, Papier auf Leinwand, 54,5 x 44,5 cm. London, The National Gallery. Inv. Nr. 1400

*Ecce homo,* 1634, Papier op dock, 54,5 x 44,5 cm. Londen, The National Gallery. Inv. Nr. 1400

*Ecce homo,* 1634, Papier marouflé sur toile, 54,5 x 44,5 cm. Londres, The National Gallery. inv. n°. 1400

**D**

*The Three Crosses,* 1653, dry-point, 38.5 x 45 cm. London, British Museum.

*Die drei Kreuze,* 1653, Kalt-nadel, 38,5 x 45 cm. London, British Museum.

*Die drie kruisen,* 1653, Droge naald, 38,5 x 45 cm. Londen, British Museum.

*Les Trois Croix,* 1653, Pointe sèche et burin, 38,5 x 45 cm. Londres, British Museum.

# EF

*Woman at an open Door (Hendrickje Stoffels?),* c. 1656-57, Canvas, 88.5 x 67 cm. Berlin, Staatliche Museen Preussischer Kulturbesitz, Gemäldegalerie. Cat. No. 828 B

*Frau an einer geöffneten Tür (Hendrickje Stoffels?),* um 1656-57, Leinwand, 88,5 x 67 cm. Berlin, Staatliche Museen Preußischer Kulturbesitz, Gemäldegalerie. Kat. Nr. 828 B

*Vrouw in de deuropening (Hendrickje Stoffels?),* ca. 1656-57, Doek, 88,5 x 67 cm. Berlijn, Staatliche Museen Preussischer Kulturbesitz, Gemäldegalerie. cat. nr. 828 B

*Femme devant une porte ouverte (Hendrickje Stoffels?),* vers 1656-57, Toile,, 88,5 x 67 cm. Berlin, Staatliche Museen Preussischer Kulturbesitz, Gemäldegalerie. nᵒ. 828 B

*A Lioness devouring a Bird,* c.1638-42, Charcoal, with grey wash, heightened with white, on paper prepared with pale brown wash, 12.6 x 23.9 cm. London, British Museum. Bequeathed by Richard Payne Knight, 1824

*Löwin einen Vogel Fressend,* um 1638-42, Holzkohle, grau laviert, weiss gehöht, auf braun grundiertem Papier, 12,6 x 23,9 cm. London, British Museum. Vermächtnis Richard Payne Knight, 1824

*Een leeuwin die een vogel verslindt,* ca.1638-42, Houtskool, grijs gewassen, met wit gehoogd, op lichtbruin getint papier, 12,6 x 23,9 cm. Londen, British Museum. Legaat Richard Payne Knight, 1824

*Lionne dévorant un oiseau,* vers 1638-42, Fusain, au lavis gris avec touches de blanc, sur papier préparé, 12,6 x 23,9 cm. Londres, British Museum. Legs de Richard Payne Knight, 1824

# EF

*Belshazzar's Feast,* c. 1635, Canvas, 167 x 209 cm. London, The National Gallery. Inv. No. 6350

*Das Gastmahl des Belsazar,* um 1635, Leinwand, 167 x 209 cm. London, The National Gallery. Inv. Nr. 6350

*Het feest van koning Belsazar,* ca. 1635, Doek, 167 x 209 cm. Londen, The National Gallery. Inv. Nr. 6350

*Le Festin de Balthazar,* vers 1635, Toile, 167 x 209 cm. Londres, The National Gallery. inv n°. 6350

*The Star of the Kings,* c.1645-47, Pen and brown ink with brown wash, 20.4 x 32.3 cm. London, The British Museum Bequeathed by George Salting, 1910-2-12-189

*Der Stern am Dreikönigsa-bend,* um 1645-47, Feder mit brauner Tinte, braun laviert, 20.4 x 32,3 cm. London, The British Museum. Vermächtnis George Salting, 1910-2-12-189

*Driekoningen: het zingen met de ster,* ca.1645-47, Pen in bruin, bruin gewassen, 20,4 x 32,3 cm. Londen, The British Museum. Legaat George Salt-ing, 1910-2-12-189

*L'Étoile des rois,* vers 1645-47, Plume et encre brune au lavis brun, 20,4 x 32,3 cm. Londres, The British Museum. Legs de George Salting, 1910-2-12-189

# G

Landscape with a stone
*Bridge,* Late 1630s, Panel,
29.5 x 42.3 cm. Amsterdam,
Rijksmuseum. Inv. No. A1935

*Landschaft mit Steinbrücke,*
Ende dreißiger Jahre, Holz,
29,5 x 42,3 cm. Amsterdam,
Rijksmuseum. Inv. Nr. A1935

*Landschap met een stenen
brug,* eind jaren dertig,
Paneel, 29,5 x 42,3 cm.
Amsterdam, Rijksmuseum.
Inv. Nr. A1935

*Paysage avec un pont de
pierre,* fin des années trente,
Bois, 29,5 x 42,3 cm. Amsterdam, Rijksmuseum. inv. n⁰.
A1935

*Self-Portrait with Mouth Open,* c.1628-29, Pen and brown ink with grey wash, 12.7 x 9.5 cm. London, British Museum. Bequeathed by C.M. Cracherode, 1799

*Selbtbildnis mit offenem Mund,* um 1628-29, Feder mit brauner Tinte, grau laviert, 12,7 x 9,5 cm. London, British Museum. Vermächtnis C.M. Cracherode, 1799

*Zelfportret met open mond,* ca.1628-29, Pen in bruin, grijs gewassen, 12,7 x 9,5 cm. Londen, British Museum. Legaat C.M. Cracherode, 1799

*Autoportrait avec bouche ouverte,* vers 1628-29, Plume et encre brune au lavis gris, 12,7 x 9,5 cm. Londres, British Museum. Legs de C.M. Cracherode, 1799

# H

H

*Three Studies of an Old Man playing with a Child,* c.1640, Pen and brown ink, touched with brown wash, on paper washed pale brown, 18.9 x 15,7 cm, London British Museum. Bequeathed by George Salting, 1910-2-12-185

*Drei Studien von einem alten Mann der mit einem Kind spielt,* um 1640, Feder mit brauner Tinte, braun laviert, auf braun grundiertem Papier, 18,9 x 15,7 cm, London, British Museum. Vermächtnis George Salting, 1910-2-12-185

*Drie studies van een oude man spelend met een kind,* ca.1640, Pen in bruin, een weinig penseel in bruine was, op lichtbruin getint papier, 18,9 x 15,7 om, Londen, British Museum. Legaat George Salting, 1910-2-12-185

*Trois études d'un vieillard jouant avec un enfant,* vers 1640, Plume et encre brune, rehaussé de lavis brun, sur papier lavé brun, 18,9 x 15,7 cm. Londres, British Museum. Legs de George Salting, 1910-2-12-185

# IJ

The Artist in his Studio,
c.1629, Panel, 25 x 32 cm.
Boston, Museum of Fine Arts.
Acc. No. 38.1838.

*Der Künstler in seiner Werk-
statt,* um 1629, Holz, 25 x 32
cm. Boston, Museum of Fine
Arts. Akz. Nr. 38.1838.

*De kunstenaar in zijn atelier,*
ca.1629, Paneel, 25 x 32 cm.
Boston, Museum of Fine Arts.
Acc. Nr. 38.1838

*Le Peintre dans son Atelier,*
vers 1629, Bois, 25 x 32 cm.
Boston, Museum of Fine Arts.
n⁰. 38.1838

*A Coach,* c.1660-63, Pen and brown ink with greyish brown wash, 19.3 x 25.4 cm. London, British Museum. Bequeathed by Richard Payne Knight, 1824

*Eine Kutsche,* um 1660-63, Feder mit brauner Tinte, mit grau-braun laviert, 19,3 x 25,4 cm. London, British Museum. Vermächtnis Richard Payne Knight, 1824

*Een karos,* ca.1660-63, Pen in bruin, grijs-bruin gewassen, 19,3 x 25,4 cm. Londen, British Museum. Legaat Richard Payne Knight, 1824

*Un Carrosse,* vers 1660-63, Plume et encre brune, au lavis brun-grisâtre, 19,3 x 25,4 cm. Londres, British Museum. Legs de Richard Payne Knight, 1824

# K

*Portrait of the Artist aged about 23*, c.1629, Panel, 37.9 x 28.9 cm. The Hague, Royal Picture Gallery, Mauritshuis. Inv. No. 148

*Selbstbildnis im Alter von ungefähr 23 Jahren,* um 1629, Holz, 37,9 x 28,9 cm. Den Haag, Koninklijk Kabinet van Schilderijen, Mauritshuis. Inv. Nr. 148

*Zelfportret op ongeveer 23-jarige leeftijd,* ca.1629, Paneel, 37,9 x 28,9 cm. Den Haag, Koninklijk Kabinet van Schilderijen, Mauritshuis. Inv. Nr. 148

*Autoportrait vers l'âge de vingt-trois ans,* vers 1629, Bois, 37,9 x 28,9 cm. La Haye, Koninklijk Kabinet van Schilderijen, Mauritshuis. n°. 148

*The Entombment of Christ
(over the Raising of Lazarus),*
c.1635, Red chalk, corrected
with white, 28.2 x 20.4 cm.
London, British Museum.
Bequeathed by William Fawkener, 1769

*Die Grablegung Christi (über
der Auferweckung des
Lazarus),* um 1635, Rote
Kreide, überarbeitet mit
weiss, 20,2 x 20,4 cm. London, British Museum.
Vermächtnis William Faw-
kener, 1769

*De graflegging (over de
opwekking van Lazarus),*
ca.1635, Roodkrijt, met wit
gecorrigeerd, 28,2 x 20,4 cm.
Londen, British Museum.
Legaat William Fawkener,
1769

*La Mise au tombeau du
Christ et la Résurrection de
Lazare surimposée,* vers
1635, Craie rouge, corrigé
avec du blanc, 28,2 x 20,4
cm. Londres, British Mus-
eum. Legs de William Faw-
kener, 1769

# L

**Susanna and the Elders,**
1647, Mahogany, 76.6 x 92.8
cm. Berlin, Staatliche Museen
Preussischer Kulturbesitz,
Gemäldegalerie. Cat. 828 E

*Susanna und die beiden Alten,* 1647, Mahagoniholz,
76,6 x 92,8 cm. Berlin, Staatliche Museen Preußischer
Kulturbesitz, Gemäldegalerie.
Kat. Nr. 828 E

*Suzanna en de twee oudsten,*
1647, Paneel (mahonie), 76,6
x 92,8 cm. Berlijn, Staatliche
Museen Preussischer Kulturbesitz, Gemäldegalerie. Cat.
828 E

*Suzanne et les vieillards,*
1647, Bois d'acajou, 76,6 x
92,8 cm. Berlin, Staatliche
Museen Preussischer
Kulturbesitz, Gemäldegalerie.
nᵒ. 828 E

*St. Jerome reading in an Italian Landscape,* c.1652, Etching, 26 x 20.7 cm. London, British Museum.

*St. Jérôme lesend in einer italienischen Landschaft,* um 1652, Radierung, 26 x 20,7 cm, London, British Museum.

*De heilige Hieronymus lezend in een Italiaans landschap,* ca.1652, Ets, 26 x 20,7 cm. Londen, British Museum.

*St. Jérôme dans un paysage italien,* vers 1652, Eau-forte, 26 x 20,7 cm. Londres, British Museum.

# L

*Lucretia,* 1666, Canvas, 105.09 x 92.29 cm. Minneapolis, The Minneapolis Institute of Arts. The William Hood Dunwoody Fund, Acc. No. 34.19

*Lucrezia,* 1666, Leinwand, 105,09 x 92,29 cm. Minneapolis, The Minneapolis Institute of Arts. The William Hood Dunwoody Fund, Akz. Nr. 34.19

*Lucretia,* 1666, Doek, 105,09 x 92,29 cm. Minneapolis, The Minneapolis Institute of Arts. The William Hood Dunwoody Fund, Acc. Nr. 34.19

*Lucrèce,* 1666, Toile, 105,09 x 92,29 cm. Minneapolis, The Minneapolis Institute of Arts. The William Hood Dunwoody Fund, nᵒ. 34.19

*Sketch of the Artist's Wife, Saskia,* c.1637, Etching, 12.7 x 10.2 cm. London, British Museum.

*Skizze der Frau des Künstlers, Saskia,* um 1637, Radierung, 12,7 x 10,2 cm. London, British Museum.

*Schets van Saskia van Uylenburgh, Rembrandt's vrouw,* ca.1637, Ets, 12,7 x 10,2 cm. Londen, British Museum.

*Étude de Saskia, femme de l'artiste,* vers 1637, Eau-forte, 12,7 x 10,2 cm. Londres, British Museum.

# M

*Titus at his Desk,* 1655, Canvas, 77 x 63 cm. Rotterdam, Museum Boymans-van Beuningen. Inv. No. St.2

*Titus an seinem Schreibpult,* 1655, Leinwand, 77 x 63 cm. Rotterdam, Museum Boymans-van Beuningen. Inv. Nr. St.2

*Titus aan zijn lezenaar,* 1655, Doek, 77 x 63 cm. Rotterdam, Museum Boymans-van Beuningen. Inv. Nr. St.2

*Titus à son pupitre,* 1655, Toile, 77 x 63 cm. Rotterdam, Museum Boymans-van Beuningen. inv. nᵒ. St.2

**M**

The Last Supper, after Leonardo da Vinci, c.1635, Red
chalk, heightened with white,
12.5 x 21 cm. London,
British Museum. Presented by
Miss Kate Radford, 1900 6 11 7

Das Abendmahl nach Leon-
ardo da Vinci, um 1635, Rote
Kreide, weiss gehöht, 12,5 x
21 cm. London, British
Museum. Geschenk von Miss
Kate Radford, 1900 6 11 7

Het laatste avondmaal, naar
Leonardo da Vinci, ca.1635,
Rood krijt, met wit gehoogd,
12,5 x 21 cm. Londen,
British Museum. Geschonken
door Miss Kate Radford, 1900,
6-11-7

La Dernier Cène: d'aprés
Léonard de Vinci, vers 1635,
Craie rouge, rehaussé de
blanc, 12,5 x 21 cm. Londres,
British Museum. Don
Miss Kate Radford 1900-6-11-7

# N

Jeremiah lamenting the Destruction of Jerusalem, 1630, Panel, 58.3 x 46.6 cm. Amsterdam, Rijksmuseum. Inv. No. A3276

Jeremias trauert über die Zerstörung Jerusalems, 1630, Holz, 58,3 x 46,6 cm. Amsterdam, Rijksmuseum. Inv. Nr. A3276

De profeet Jeremia treurend over de verwoesting van Jeruzalem, 1630, Paneel, 58,3 x 46,6 cm. Amsterdam, Rijksmuseum. Inv. Nr. A3276

Le Prophète Jérémie pleurant la destruction de Jérusalem, 1630, Bois, 58,3 x 46,6 cm. Amsterdam, Rijksmuseum. inv. n⁰. A3276

N

Four Orientals seated under
a Tree, c.1656-61, Pen and
brown ink with brown and
grey wash, touched with
white, 19.4 x 12.4 cm. London British Museum.
1895-9-15-1275

*Vier unter einem Baum sit-
zenden Sheiks, nach einer
indischen Miniatur des sieb-
zehnten Jahrhunderts,* um
1656-61, Feder mit brauner
Tinte, braun und grau laviert,
weiss gehöht, 19,4 x 12,4 cm.
London, British Museum.
1895-9-15-1275

*Vier sjeiks zittend onder een
boom, naar een zeventiende-
eeuwse Indiase miniatuur,*
ca.1656-61, Pen in bruin,
bruin en grijs gewassen, met
wit gehoogd, 19,4 x 12,4 cm.
Londen, British Museum.
1895-9-15-1275

*Quatre Orientaux assis sous
un arbre,* vers 1656-61, Plume
et encre brune au lavis brun et
gris, avec touches de blanc,
19,4 x 12,4 cm. Londres,
British Museum. 1895-9-15-
1275

# N

*Self-Portrait*, c.1665, Canvas, 114.3 x 94 cm. London, Kenwood. Iveagh Bequest, Inv. No. 57

*Selbstbildnis,* um 1665, Leinwand, 114,3 x 94 cm. London Kenwood. Iveagh Bequest, Inv. Nr. 57

*Zelfportret,* ca.1665, Doek, 114,3 x 94 cm. Londen, Kenwood. Iveagh Bequest. Inv. Nr. 57

*Autoportrait,* vers 1665, Toile, 114,3 x 94 cm. Londres, Kenwood. Legs Iveagh, inv. n°. 57

*The Lamentation at the Foot of the Cross,* c.1634-35, Pen and brown ink with brown wash, with red and perhaps some black chalk, reworked in oil-paint en grisaille, 21.6 x 25.4 cm. London, British Museum. Bequeathed by Richard Payne Knight, 1824

*Die Wehklage am Fuß des Kreuzes,* um 1634-35, Feder mit brauner Tinte, mit roter und vielleicht etwas schwarzer Kreide, überarbeitet Ölfarbe en grisaille 21,6 x 25,4 cm. London, British Museum. Vermächtnis Richard Payne Knight, 1824

*De bewening aan de voet van het kruis,* ca.1634-35, Pen in bruin, bruin gewassen, rood en misschien wat zwart krijt, bewerkt met olieverf, 21,6 x 25,4 cm. Londen, British Museum. Legaat Richard Payne Knight, 1824

*Lamentation au pied de la Croix,* vers 1634-35, Plume et encre brune au lavis brun, avec craie noire et peut-être un peu de craie rouge, retravaillé à l'huile en grisaille, 21,6 x 25,4 cm. Londres, British Museum. Legs de Richard Payne Knight, 1824

# O

*A Woman Bathing,* 1654,
Oak panel, 61.8 x 47 cm. London, The National Gallery.
Inv. No. 54

*Badende Frau,* 1654, Eichenholz, 61,8 x 47 cm. London, The National Gallery. Inv. Nr. 54

*Badende vrouw,* 1654, Paneel (eikehout), 61,8 x 47 cm. Londen, The National Gallery. Inv. Nr. 54

*Jeune femme au bain,* 1654, Bois de chêne, 61,8 x 47 cm. Londres, The National Gallery. inv. n°. 54

*Christ and St. Peter on the Sea of Galilee,* c.1652-56, Reed pen and brown ink, touched with white, 19.1 x 29.1 cm. London, British Museum. Bequeathed by George Salting, 1910-2-12-180

*Christus und St. Peter auf der Sea von Galilea,* um 1652-56, Schilf-Rohr Feder mit brauner Tinte, weiss gehöht, 19,1 x 29,1 cm. London, British Museum. Vermächtnis George Salting, 1910-2-12-180

*Christus en Petrus op het meer van Galilea,* ca.1652-56, Rietpen in bruin, met wit gehoogd, 19,1 x 29,1 cm. Londen, British Museum. Legaat George Salting, 1910-2-12-180

*Le Christ et St. Pierre sur la mer de Galilée,* vers 1652-56, Plume de roseau et encre brune, rehaussé de blanc, 19,1 x 29,1 cm. Londres, British Museum. Legs de George Salting, 1910-2-12-180

# PQ

*Flora,* 1635, Canvas, 123.7 x 97.5 cm. London, The National Gallery. Inv. No. 4930

*Flora,* 1635, Leinwand, 123,7 x 97,5 cm. London, The National Gallery. Inv. Nr. 4930

*Flora,* 1635, Doek, 123,7 x 97,5 cm. Londen, The National Gallery. Inv. Nr. 4930

*Saskia en Flore,* 1635, Toile, 123,7 x 97,5 cm. Londres, The National Gallery. inv. n⁰. 4930

R

The Holy Family in the
Carpenter's Workshop,
c.1645, Pen and brown ink
with brown wash, touched
with white, 18.4 x 24.6 cm.
London, British Museum.
Bequeathed by Henry Vau-
ghan, 1900-8-24-144

Die heilige Familie in einer
Zimmerwerkstatt, um 1645,
Feder mit brauner Tinte,
braun laviert, weiss gehöht,
18,4 x 24,6 cm. London,
British Museum. Vermächtnis
Henry Vaughan, 1900-8-24-
144

De Heilige Familie in de tim-
merwerkplaats, ca.1645, Pen
in bruin, bruin gewassen, met
wit gehoogd, 18,4 x 24,6 cm.
Londen, British Museum.
Legaat Henry Vaughan, 1900-
8-24-144

La Sainte Famille dans
l'atelier du charpentier, vers
1645, Plume et encre brune,
rehaussé de blanc, 18,4 x 24,6
cm. Londres, British Mus-
eum. Legs de Henry Vaughan,
1900 0 24-144

# R

*Self-Portrait,* 1669, Canvas, 63.5 x 57.8 cm. The Hague, Mauritshuis. Inv. No. 840

*Selbstbildnis,* 1669, Leinwand, 63,5 x 57,8 cm. Den Haag, Mauritshuis. Inv. Nr. 840

*Zelfportret,* 1669, Doek, 63,5 x 57,8 cm. Den Haag, Mauritshuis. Inv. Nr. 840

*Autoportrait,* 1669, Toile, 63,5 x 57,8 cm. La Haye, Mauritshuis. inv. n°. 840

*The Three Trees*, 1643, Etching, 21.1 x 28 cm. London, British Museum.

*Die drei Bäume*, 1643, Radierung, 21,1 x 28 cm. London, British Museum.

*De drie bomen*, 1643, Ets, 21,1 x 28 cm. Londen, British Museum.

*Paysage aux trois arbres*, 1643, Eau-forte, 21,1 x 28 cm Londres, British Museum.

# S

*John the Baptist preaching,* c. 1634-35, Canvas on panel, 62.7 x 81 cm. Berlin, Staatliche Museen Preussischer Kulturbesitz, Gemäldegalerie. Cat. No. 828 K

*Die Predigt Johannes des Taüfers,* um 1634-35, Leinwand auf Tafel, 62,7 x 81 cm. Berlin, Staatliche Museen Preußischer Kulturbesitz, Gemäldegalerie. Kat. Nr. 828 K

*Die prediking van Johannes de Doper,* ca. 1634-35, Doek op paneel, 62,7 x 81 cm. Berlijn, Staatliche Museen Preussischer Kulturbesitz, Gemäldegalerie. cat. nr. 828 K

*La Prédication de saint Jean-Baptiste,* vers 1634-35, Toile,, 62,7 x 81 cm. Berlin, Staatliche Museen Preussischer Kulturbesitz, Gemäldegalerie. n⁰. 828 K

S

*Christ preaching: The Hun-dred Guilder Print,* c.1642-49, Etching, 27.8 x 38.9 cm. London, British Museum.

*Christus predigend: Das Hundertguldenblatt,* um 1642-49, Radierung, 27,8 x 38,9 cm. London, British Museum.

*De hunderd guldensprent,* ca.1642-49, Ets, 27,8 x 38,9 cm. Londen, British Museum.

*Le Christ prechant: La Pièce de cent florins,* vers 1642-49, Eau-forte, 27,8 x 38,9 cm. Londres, British Museum.

# S

*An Elephant,* c.1637, Black chalk and charcoal, 17.9 x 25.6 cm. London, British Museum. Bequeathed by C. M, Cracherode, 1799

*Ein Elephant,* um 1637, Schwarze Kreide und Holzkohle, 17,9 x 25,6 cm. London, British Museum. Vermächtnis C.M. Cracherode, 1799

*Een olifant,* ca.1637, Zwart krijt en houtskool, 17,9 x 25,6 cm. Londen, British Museum. Legaat C.M. Cracherode, 1799

*Un Éléphant,* vers 1637, Craie noire et fusain, 17,9 x 25,6 cm. Londres, British Museum. Legs de C.M. Cracherode, 1799

T

*Susanna and the Elders,*
1636, Panel, 47.2 x 38.6 cm.
The Hague, Royal Picture Gallery, Mauritshuis. Inv. No.
147

*Susanna und die beiden
Alten,* 1636, Holz, 47,2 x 38,6
cm. Den Haag, Koninklijk
Kabinet van Schilderijen,
Mauritshuis. Inv. Nr. 147

*Suzanna en de ouderlingen,*
1636, Paneel, 47,2 x 38,6 cm.
Den Haag, Koninklijk Kabinet
van Schilderijen, Mauritshuis.
Inv. Nr. 147

*Suzanne au bain,* 1636, Bois,
47,2 x 38,6 cm. La Haye,
Koninklijk Kabinet van Schilderijen, Mauritshuis. inv. n°.
147

Landscape: The Bend in the
Amstel River at Kostverloren,
c.1650, Reed pen and brown
ink with brown wash,
touched with white, on paper
prepared with brown wash.
14.5 x 21.3 cm. London,
British Museum. 1984-11-10-9

Landschaft: Die Biegung des
Amstel Flusses bei Kostverloren, um 1650, Schilf-Rohr
Feder mit brauner Tinte,
braun laviert, weiss gehöht,
auf braun grundiertem Papier,
14,5 x 21,3 cm. London,
British Museum. 1984-11-10-9

Landschap: bocht in de
Amstel bij Kostverloren,
ca.1650, Rietpen in bruin,
bruin gewassen, met wit
gehoogd, op bruin getint
papier, 14,5 x 21,3 cm.
London, British Museum
1984-11-10-9

Paysage: méandre du fleuve
de l'Amstel à Kostverloren,
vers 1650, Plume, encre
brune, lavis brun, avec
touches de blanc, sur papier
préparé avec du lavis brun,
14,5 x 21,3 cm. Londres,
British Museum. 1984-11-10-9

# UV

The Virgin and Child seated by a Window, c.1634-35, Pen and brown ink with brown wash, 15.5 x 13.8 cm. London, British Museum. Purchased, 1859-8-6-2

*Maria mit Kind am Fenster sitzend,* um 1634 35, Feder mit brauner Tinte, braun laviert, 15,5 x 13,8 cm. London, British Museum. Erworben, 1859-8-6-2

*Maria en het kind Jezus zittend bij een raam,* ca.1634-35, Pen in bruin, bruin gewassen, 15,5 x 13,8 cm. Londen, British Museum. Verworven 1859-8-6-2

*La Vierge et l'enfant assis à une fenêtre,* vers 1634-35, Plume et encre brune au lavis brun, 15,5 x 13,8 cm. Londres, British Museum. Achat, 1859-8-6-2

# W

*Portrait of Agatha Bas*, 1641, Canvas, 104 x 82 cm. London, Buckingham Palace. Collection of H.M. Queen Elizabeth II. Inv. nº. 1157

*Bildnis der Agatha Bas*, 1641, Leinwand, 104 x 82 cm. London, Buckingham Palace. Sammlung Ihrer Majestät Königin Elisabeth II. Inv. Nr. 1157

*Portret van Agatha Bas*, 1641, Doek, 104 x 82 cm. Londen, Buckingham Palace. Verzameling H.M. Koningin Elizabeth II. Inv. Nr. 1157

*Portrait d'Agatha Bas, femme de Nicolaes van Bambeeck*, 1641, Toile, 104 x 82 cm. Londres, Buckingham Palace. Collection de Sa Majesté Elisabeth II. Inv. nº. 1157

Hendrickje Stoffels sleeping, c.1654, Drawn with the brush and brown wash, with some white bodycolour. 24.6 x 20.3 cm. London, British Museum. 1895-9-15-1279

Hendrickje Stoffels schlafend, um 1654, Pinselzeichnung auf braun Laviertem Papier, mit etwas weißer Farbe, 24,6 x 20,3 cm. London, British Museum. 1895-9-15-1279

Hendrickje Stoffels slapend, ca.1654, Penseel in bruin, bruin gewassen, met wit gehoogd 24,6 x 20,3 cm. Londen, British Museum. 1895-9-15-1279

Hendrickje Stoffels endormie, vers 1654, Dessiné au pinceau et au lavis brun, avec de la gouache blanche, 24,6 x 20,3 cm. Londres, British Museum. 1895-9-15-1279

# XYZ

Portrait of the Artist Jacques
de Gheyn III, 1632, Panel,
29.9 x 24.9 cm. London, Dulwich Picture Gallery. Cat. No.
99

*Bildnis des Malers Jacques de
Gheyn III*, 1632, Holz, 29,9 x
24,9 cm. London, Dulwich
Picture Gallery. Cat. Nr. 99

*Portret van de schilder Jac-
ques de Gheyn III*, 1632,
Paneel, 29,9 x 24,9 cm.
Londen, Dulwich Picture Gallery. Kat. Nr. 99

*Portrait du peintre Jacob de
Gheyn III*, 1632, Bois, 29,9 x
24,9 cm. Londres, Dulwich
Picture Gallery. n°. 99

*Esau selling his Birthright to Jacob,* c.1640-41, Pen and brown ink, with greyish brown wash mixed with some white heightening, 20 x 17.4 cm. London, British Museum. Bequeathed by C. M. Cracherode, 1799

*Esau verkauft seine Erstgeburt an Jacob,* um 1640-41, Feder mit brauner Tinte, mit grau-braun laviert, gemischte mit etwas weiss gehöht, 20 x 17,4 cm. London, British Museum. Vermächtnis C.M. Cracherode, 1799

*Esau verkoopt zijn geboorterecht aan Jacob,* ca.1640-41, Pen in bruin, grijs-bruin gew assen, met wit gehoogd, 20 x 17,4 cm. Londen, British Museum. Legaat C.M. Cracherode, 1799

*Esau vendant son droit d'ainesse à Jacob,* vers 1640-41, Plume et encre brune, au lavis brun-grisâtre mélangé avec des touches de blanc, 20 x 17,4 cm. Londres, British Museum. Legs de C.M. Cracherode, 1799

# XYZ

*Portrait of Saskia van Uylenburgh*, 1633, Silverpoint on white prepared parchment, 18.5 x 10.7 cm. Berlin, Staatliche Museen Preussicher Kulturbesitz, Kupferstichkabinett.

*Bildnis Saskia van Uylenburgh*, 1633, Silberstift auf weiß präpariertem Pergament, 18,5 x 10,7 cm. Berlin, Staatliche Museen Preußicher Kulturbesitz, Kupferstichkabinett.

*Portret van Saskia van Uylenburgh*, 1647, Zilverstift op wit geprepareerd perkament, 18,5 x 10,7 cm. Berlin, Staatliche Museen Preussicher Kulturbesitz, Kupferstichkabinett.

*Portrait de Saskia van Uylenburgh*, 1633, Pointe d'argent sur vélin blanc, 18,5 x 10,7 cm. Berlin, Staatliche Museen Preussicher Kulturbesitz, Kupferstichkabinett.